Copyright © Michael Kewley 2020
ISBN: 978-1-899417-23-0
Published by:
Panna Dipa Books.
e-mail: dhammateacher@hotmail.com

Format and cover photograph © Isabelle Kewley 2020

Summary

DHAMMA IN YOUR POCKET

by
Michael Kewley
Dhammachariya Paññadipa

Introduction

The essence of Dhamma practice is to stay in balance and not be pulled out into the vicissitudes of life. This of course is easier said than done as the demands that we meet in life rarely become less and so it is not uncommon to find our Dhamma practice pushed into second or third place simply because of time constraints and family or other obligations. However, now we can reach into our pocket for this small book and be reminded of what has true value and what does not, and where to put our attention. Sitting retreats and visiting the teacher will always be the highest form of practice but when that is not possible, we will still have the words of the Master to inspire us to stay in our centre. Simple reminders or moments of reflection, these few pages are a gift for the heart.

May all beings be happy.

It is only from the centre
that we can see the periphery.

Part 1.

MEDITATION & PRACTICE

Whatever mental projections you may make about your practice and your goals for self improvement, you can only ever train yourself in the moment.

So, when anger, frustration, bitterness, anxiety etc, arise, you have not failed, it is simply the opportunity to practice. To see this moment, to accept it as it is, and to let go of your attachment to it as being right or wrong. Now is the moment to see it as the opportunity for your own liberation.

We do not need to free ourselves from the world and what it presents, only from our attachment to the mind and its endless approval and disapproval as being right or wrong!

This is how to use daily life as your Dhamma path.

May all beings be happy.

1.

Live with love and be aware,
nothing has greater value than this.

2.

Do what you're supposed to do
and don't let this mind trick you
into giving up.

3.

If you really want to be happy,
look at the cause of your unhappiness,
it's much more subtle than you might think.

4.

There are no teachers of enlightenment,
there is only the sharing of Dhamma.

5.

Boredom is such a wonderful thing
to look at in your meditation,
because it's such a dangerous thing
to have in your life.

6.

The obstacle to our enlightenment
is only the mind
that wants to be enlightened.

7.

Patience in life
is not the same experience
as waiting for something.

8.

If you cannot be quiet,
if you cannot be still,
how will you ever hear your heart?

9.

Dhamma teachings are not personal,
but they are always about you.

10.

It is impatience
that becomes the obstacle.

11.

The difference between
'tell me the Truth'
and 'tell me what I want to hear',
is liberation.

12.

There is much more to liberation
than simply smiling at nice words
and sitting cross legged on the floor.

13.

The most disastrous thing we can do in life
is forget the importance
of our Dhamma training.

14.

Because life is short and uncertain
we must cultivate a sense of urgency
in our Dhamma training.

15.

Whatever you might think
in different moments,
anger is never your friend
and fear is never your support.

16.

If your teacher does not direct you
towards liberation,
what value do they have?

17.

Silencing the mind
and allowing the mind to fall silent
is not the same thing.

18.

You can't 'let go'.
Letting go only happens
when 'you' are not there.

19.

When it comes to Dhamma practice,
we start by stopping.

20.

Loving Kindness is not about
a good feeling in the meditation,
it is about a relationship with life.

21.

With wisdom we know
how to live for ourselves,
with love we do not insist
that others follow our way.

22.

We can't share joy
with those who are angry.
Better to stay in a loving silence.

23.

Wherever you are,
the Dhamma is there.

24.

If people truly understood
the reality of Kamma,
they would take much greater care
with their lives.

25.

Don't be too much owned
by the things you think you own.

26.

It is by holding on to life
that we fear death.
It is by holding on to the past
that we fear the future.

27.

There is no reward
to your Dhamma practice,
only the beautiful consequence of it.

28.

Better not to carry the bad behaviour of others
and so allow it to influence your own behaviour.
This is not the way to peace.

29.

Work hard
and go deep in your understanding.

30.

If you don't know what forms the waves
how will you ever understand the ocean?

31.

The essence of Dhamma practice
is not to believe anything.

32.

Sit quietly, live lovingly, and serve all beings.
This is the way to peace.

33.

Our practice is not to become happier,
but to understand the cause
of our unhappiness.

34.

We cannot force the mind into silence,
but with wisdom and patience
we can allow the mind to fall silent.

35.

Our practice is not to become someone special
but only to serve others with love.

36.

When possessiveness for things falls away,
our personal world will find
its own beautiful balance.

37.

The moment you stop insisting
how everything should be,
your struggle with life will simply fall away.
Now you will respond from love,
rather than react through fear.

38.

Life is not always easy, but it's always the Path.

39.

Only when you awaken from the dream will
you know you have been asleep.

40.

When there is no more fascination
with meditation,
our Dhamma work can truly begin.

41.

Your practice isn't only about you
sitting in meditation,
it's about all the times
when you're not sitting in meditation.

42.

The things that disturb you in life
are the true gifts to your practice.

43.

You're everywhere except in the moment.

44.

Cultivate a loving patience in your practice.
Do what you should do
with a graceful gentleness and compassion.
Things of value should not be forced.

45.

The truth is not an opinion or a belief.
It cannot be found by shouting and argument,
but in the silence of meditation
and a simple living compassion.

46.

It is the peaceful mind that says,
'no matter how bad your behavior is,
it will not dictate mine'.

47.

Our practice is not to create
a special spiritual state to hold on to,
but simply let go of the obstacles
to the purity within.

48.

This morning it rained.
This afternoon it is sunny.
How is that not like the mind?

49.

We can only let go of the different
manifestations of our desires and fears
when they appear in front of us.

50.

The moment we make
the cultivation of love and awareness
the most important thing in our life,
we will find our way
to peace, harmony and freedom.

51.

Without our suffering,
how can we be free from our suffering?

Dhamma in your pocket

Part 2.

LOVE & FEAR

The amount of fear you carry will determine the amount of anger and intolerance you project into the world. Reflect on this it's important.

No matter how much you can shout and be insensitive to others, no matter how you can then cleverly explain and justify your conduct, in front of the awakened heart, you are always seen and known.

Love smiles, fear scowls, and so you will never find peace in your life until the fear you carry is ended and the loving fearless heart manifests.

This is the way of Dhamma.

May all beings be happy.

52.

It is only love
that will save you from yourself.

53.

In the end, if it's not love,
it's not anything at all.

54.

In order to be free,
you must cultivate love
for that which makes you afraid.

55.

No-one can make you happy
and no-one can make you unhappy,
it just seems like that
when you are asleep.

56.

Peace begins and ends with love.

57.

Love is the environment
where you are no longer
afraid of your fear.

58.

Love means to accept this being
as being this being.

59.

Liking and disliking are personal things,
but love is universal.

60.

Behind all the things
that really don't matter
we are all exactly the same.
Knowing this is love.

61.

One thing is certain,
hatred and violence
will not take you to peace.

62.

It is only the mind that divides the world,
the heart sees love everywhere.

63.

What we call 'life' is always about a moment.
A moment of love, or a moment of fear.

64.

The moment you have love for you,
is the moment you have love for all beings.

65.

As each breath is a new breath,
each moment is a new moment
and so the opportunity to share
your loving heart is always present.

66.

If you don't have love for yourself,
what is it that you will share with others?

67.

Our life is always better
when it's established in love.

68.

When everything is love,
there is no love,
there is only this.

69.

You may be deeply involved in your religion,
but love and a living compassion for all beings
is much more important.

70.

When fear is finished
there are no more problems to be resolved,
only life to be lived.

71.

In the end, kindness is everything.

72.

In the place where Dhamma is alive
there is enough of everything for all beings.
In the place where Dhamma is dead
there is only greed and fear.

73.

Love is not an idea,
it is an action.

74.

Your fears won't protect you,
and your desires will not fulfil you.
Only love will serve you
and bring joy into your life.

75.

When the basis
for all our worldly actions is love,
how can we fail?

76.

How can I offer you
anything more beautiful,
than to love you
and want nothing in return?

77.

Whatever you think,
and no matter how much you can justify it,
your fear is not helping the situation.

78.

When the heart is open,
you never have to remember to be kind.

79.

Continually empowering your weakness
does not make you stronger.

80.

We are always prisoners
to our fear and anger.
Freedom comes only through love.

81.

Life is very simple,
we either help each other or we don't
and if we don't, we need to look deep inside
ourselves and ask why?

82.

Fear is always your weakness.
Love is always your strength.

83.

When the heart is open,
love, infinite compassion
and caring for others,
is no longer a choice.
It is the only reality.

84.

The greatest gift we can give,
is to love without conditions.

85.

Make love the foundation of your life
and share the most beautiful part of you
with the world.

86.

Whatever the situation, love is the answer,
because the loving heart
can never be defeated.

87.

If you truly understood the power of love,
fear would have no place in your heart.

88.

Love is more than a smile on the face,
it is an open-hearted relationship with life.

89.

If we do not serve all beings with a loving heart,
what do we really contribute to the world?
What enduring value will our life have?

90.

The moment you have love for you,
is the moment you have love for all beings.

Dhamma in your pocket

Part 3.

INTEGRITY & LIVING

If life was so easy, no one would struggle.

If relationships were so simple, no one would suffer.

Finding a clear path through life is our Dhamma journey.

Putting down the conditions we impose upon the universe is freedom.

Nothing is ever out of place and with the heart open, everything is a gift.

May all beings be happy.

91.

Cultivating awareness and love for all beings
is the true manifestation of Dhamma.

92.

It is the quality of the mind states you empower
that determines your happiness.

93.

When we turn to the pure Dhamma path
with integrity and determination,
blessings appear daily.

94.

I do not want to be told how to live
by those I believe
to be less wise than me.

95.

It is your integrity and your kindness
that make the world beautiful.

96.

Those who kill, support, or encourage
others to violence cannot avoid the kammic
consequences of their actions,
no matter what they do.

97.

The difference between service
and power is integrity.

98.

Always reflect upon all your motivations.

99.

In the whole history of life,
fear, hatred and anger
are the three conditions of mind
that have never brought a worthy solution
to any difficulty.

100.

It is easy to sound wise
whilst talking about someone else's life.

101.

If you really think
that your purpose in life
is to convince everyone else
that you are always right,
something is very wrong!

102.

Agreeing or disagreeing
has nothing to do with Truth.

103.

Happiness is always close
when our pleasures are simple.

104.

It is true that we have no real control,
but we always have the opportunity
to respond wisely to everything we meet.

105.

It is the language we use
that determines our relationship
to the situation.

106.

It's always up to you,
how you meet your life
and how you respond.

107.

Compromise begins
when your need to be liked is greater
than your desire to be authentic.

108.

Only those truly committed to the Path
are brave enough to put down
the cause of their suffering.

109.

True freedom arises
when you do not want anything
from anyone else.

110.

We show only our own inadequacy
when we try to impose
our personal views on others.

111.

If your path is not directed by kindness,
what are you really bringing to the world?

112.

Awakened or not,
we are still left caring for this body.

113.

All beings deserve our love and respect,
but not all beings deserve us in their life.

114.

Each of us is alone
and that aloneness is tempered
by our open loving heart
or our fearful, greed based mind.
We each make our own world.

115.

To be nobody sharing your heart
is many times greater
than being somebody preaching your religion.

116.

We may argue to keep them,
but the obstacles to our liberation
are always desire and fear.

117.

How can we ever feel comfortable
when we see fear
in the eyes of a fellow being?

118.

Our problem is not that life is like this,
our problem is that we want it to be different.

119.

Life isn't really about how much you know;
it's about how you can live in the world
without making everything
that happens about you.

120.

We don't need to save ourselves from the world,
only from ourselves and the stories we create.

121.

Gender, culture or colour
is never a reason to judge another.

122.

With fear you cannot see,
with hatred you cannot hear,
with anger you cannot be compassionate.

123.

With awareness we see.
With love we accept.
With wisdom we respond.
This is the whole of Dhamma.

124.

Those who seek power
will use even the smallest thing
to divide the world.
Trust only your own heart.

Part 4.

UNDERSTANDING & SELF

Many people are attracted to meditation and a so called spiritual life, provided it feeds the ego, but this is not our way.

Our way of Pure Dhamma is to become less and less until we are like the wind in the trees or the ripples on the water, in reality only a beautiful movement of love, compassion and joy seeking nothing for itself but serving the world with kindness.

Letting go of the ever demanding ego (self-identity) is the greatest gift we can bring to our own life and the life of all beings.

The less of 'you' there is, the happier you will be.

This is how to be no-one, going no-where.

May all beings be happy.

125.

Awakening is the greatest thing
you can't imagine.

126.

To understand Dhamma
is to understand life.

127.

Being alone and being lonely
are not the same thing.

128.

Self is only a dream you are having
and Awakening, before its actual realisation
is just the same.

129.

Nothing is here to teach you anything,
it is only your heart and your wisdom
that gives things value.

130.

Where there is self
there is always division.

131.

There are no techniques in Dhamma training,
there is only the practice of awareness and love.

132.

The truth about Truth is,
it only hurts when you oppose it.

133.

When there is no grasping
at any form of happiness outside yourself,
you are free.

134.

What is important in our life
is only important
because we make it important.

135.

Of all the things that are worth having,
freedom from the needs of self
is the greatest.

136.

Not everything in life is about you,
you just make it about you.

137.

With every identity you grasp at you
separate yourself from the world of others.

138.

I tell you this simple thing,
where there is desire and fear, there is self.
Where there is self there is no freedom.

139.

Awakening is not the getting of something,
it is the putting down of everything
that takes you to suffering.

140.

When self is dissolved,
who can call themselves 'teacher'?

141.

Whatever we meet in life
only ever has the power we give it.

142.

The one called 'Master'
is simply the being in whom
Dhamma flows freely.

143.

Awakening is love,
it is the Path that cannot be taught,
only shared.

144.

How can we be free
if we only cover our old story
with a new one?

145.

Attachment is the source of the greatest
pleasure, and the greatest pain.

146.

Reflecting inwards
before looking outwards
is the way of Dhamma.

147.

Things do not happen for a reason;
things happen as a consequence
to what has gone before.

148.

You will not know your delusions
until you awaken from them.

149.

We teach what we have learned.
We share what we have understood.

150.

For every one person that hates,
there are a million that care.

151.

The place of the Master
is not to lead you to enlightenment,
but to illuminate your delusions about it.

152.

Labels on identity are convenient,
but so limiting and misleading.

153.

Life only has the shape we give it.

154.

Those seeking fame, money or sexual favours
are still trapped in the world of self.
The heart, the selfless part of us,
simply gives and shares itself
without needing to be asked in advance,
and looks for nothing in return.

155.

When Dhamma is present
there is enough for all.
When Dhamma is lost, suffering begins.

156.

When self falls away,
all divisions fall away.
Now we are one.

157.

Our beautiful loving Dhamma practice
must free us from self-identity,
not add to it.

158.

Our Dhamma life is essentially a simple affair.
To advance means to watch
our attachments gently fall away
until only the purity of being remains.

159.

In the quiet discretion of practice,
the Master sees those who are invisible.

160.

Even with their hands in Anjali,
only a few who approach the Dhamma
are ready to put down the burden of self.

161.

Only with integrity and selfless commitment
will Dhamma and its pure message of love,
compassion and wisdom
continue in the world.

162.

Freedom is not something to get,
it is something to realise.

Also by Michael Kewley

1994: Higher than Happiness (Revised edition: 2014)

1996: Vipassana, the way to an awakened life (Revised edition: 2013) - Vipassana, der Weg in ein erwachtes Leben (German version)

1999: Not This (Revised edition: 2013)

1999: Life Changing Magic (Revised edition: 2009)

2006: Walking the Path (Second Edition: 2007)

2007: The Other Shore

2009: Life is not Personal - Nimm das Leben nicht persönlich (German version)

2007: The Reality of Kamma

2011: Buttons in the Dana Box

2011: The Dhammapada

2015: Loving Awareness

2017: A journey to Awakening (autobiography)

2019: The face of Dhamma

About the author

Michael Kewley is the former Buddhist monk Paññadipa, who is now an internationally acclaimed Master of Dhamma, presenting courses and meditation retreats throughout the world. For many years he was the guiding teacher at the International Meditation Centre, Budh Gaya, India and is the founder of the Pure Dhamma tradition of spiritual Awakening.

A disciple of the late Sayadaw Rewata Dhamma, he teaches solely on the instruction of his own Master; to share the Dhamma, in the spirit of the Buddha, so that all beings might benefit. On 26th May 2002, during a special ceremony at the Dhamma Talaka Temple in England, he was awarded the title of Dhammachariya.

A full biography of Michael Kewley, including videos and Dhamma talk extracts, can be found at:

www.puredhamma.org

Dhamma in your pocket

Lightning Source UK Ltd.
Milton Keynes UK
UKHW020927271220
375968UK00010B/563